BIG ME!

BIG ME!

The dynamics of leadership

CHINEDU DARLINGTON

ACKNOWLEDGEMENT

Writing a book is actually harder than I thought but the rewards and the fulfillment it brings with it is more than I had ever imagined. I am eternally grateful to God for everything he has done for me, my family and friends. His grace and enablement was all that helped me to start and finish this work. He formed his strength in me and the people that has helped me in making this work possible. THANK YOU LORD because without you, I wouldn't be able to do any of this.

I sincerely appreciate Engr Ifechukwu Michaels for his unreserved attention and patience. He worked on this book with me and encouraged me all the way. Thank you for all the inconveniences you allowed from me. Words are not enough to tell you how much I appreciate you.

To my Nwanyioma, mara nma (beautiful woman), M'lady Chimkanma Chimnazaekpere, your immense support is everything I have ever needed. Thank you and may my God bless you (Chineke m goziere m gi).

Thanks to every other person who in one way or the other has contributed to the success of this book, my mentors, bosses, fellow coaches, contributors of all sources of information needed, you will never lose your rewards. Thank you.

TABLE OF CONTENTS

PREFACE

A leader is a servant with vision, when he sails in the euphoria of achieving his goal or goals for himself and for others...I guess I should leave you to imagine the outcome. Leadership is energy and responsibility. I have told my story in almost all the chapters in this book. The narratives of many other peoples' experiences similar to mine are also incorporated. Of course, it is sometimes a bitter truth, but I am hoping it helps others who may be thinking that they are alone. My intention is to change things that I can, but first I must learn how to change me before affecting others.

BIG ME! (The dynamics of leadership) is a clear pattern that exposes and aligns the small version of me '*Small Me*' to a continuous journey of leadership in attaining my bigger version of me, '*Big Me*'. However, '*Small Me*' grows into '*Big Me*' with determination born out of intelligence, passion, and willingness to overcome adversity. The journey is an unending journey till everyone is in the right place.

These chapters are in line with leadership characterization, narratives and stories, poems, and lots of uncommon but familiar lessons.

Leadership shows visible growth in homogeneity that is determined by events and proactive effort towards a better future

1

INTRODUCTION

I grew up in a large family and we didn't have the luxury of playing with toys and games. At that time, seeing other kids coming to school with comic books, toys and even what looks like a better snack box than mine, I always wished we were richer than we were. All those fancy displays from some of those kids gave us the impression of them being 'rich kids', and it worked because they were the popular ones. In retrospect, my family was doing fine in the context of our society back then, I can now understand that the rate of our consumption was high and income then must be managed very well to ensure longer periods of sustainability.

In our home, growing up in such a large family was challenging and at the same time fun; everything was shared, you practically had no privacy. The only privacy you had were those thoughts swinging through your mind. Even in that your moment of serenity, someone will always pry in with rhetoric concern, "what's the problem? Are you okay?" You were supposed to be fine, and if you are awfully quiet then something must be wrong; it is then assumed you must have a real problem.

In our home, it was mandatory for everyone to have a daily chore, it may be going to the farm, fetching water, mopping the floor, doing the dishes, doing laundry and I hated it. I hated doing chores! The bad news was, I did not have a choice; nobody in our house even had a choice to rogue on chores, it had to be done properly. My resentment over doing chores and yet, not having my own toy to play with always lured me out of the house. At least, I can get to play football, table tennis with my friends and some other street boys all day long. It was a form of distraction in disguise, though we were having fun while playing out there with no restrictions.

But thinking about it now, maybe it was also a form of valuable training as it exposed me to understand the street and the dynamism of our divisive world, which we all grew up in. The society's thirst for morals promotes discipline and spiritual enterprise; sadly, peer pressure promotes the opposite. This dynamism has little to do with the discipline needed to keep up and survive in this present gullible fast moving world. The society despises youthful exuberance and so does the church and other religious sects. The church is largely not a big proponent for adventures and the society feels bored listening to the church reminding us that everything under the surface of the earth is vanity. So it was, and it is still a circle of divide between the youth, the church, and the society. I grew up in this kind of divide, and all I desired was a unit of harmony that will allow me lead my life with no bias. But yet, the preacher man will always amplify my impending doom in afterlife, preying my little conscience.

The society would barricade my excesses with a code of conduct, which was attached with a punishment if I'm found wanting. Yet, my exuberance will always agitate for a liberty of expression. I know they all meant well for me, but without balance, the harmony in me will suffer. Somehow, I was living in constant fear of going to hell if I dare express my youthfulness, or going to jail for partaking in any ethical misconduct. My moral values were formidable but it didn't help me forge a balanced comprehensive development, because the realities made me lose my unbiased imaginations and creativity. It was cruelty to my young mind from my immediate environment, which may not have motivated me thereby hampering my productivity (It is simply a systematic societal deprivation of a child's right, which will result in leadership degradation in time to come).

My young mind was fragile and fertile even when deprived. Sadly, most of its conceived behaviors were viewed as irrational, unchecked, poorly motivated, and having little or no substance for conscious cognitive development and learning. Of course, every child is born with a genius but when empathy is directed further away from that child, it may tarnish his self-pride; soon inferiority complex will start rearing its head. Inferiority complex may lead to poor performance on the side of any child, and the child can become ridiculed for a choice that unconsciously took over him. In such a case, it is possible nobody will see the reason behind the child's poor performance but rather the poor results that highlights failure is what is seen...

I was that child; every African child is that child!
Any child that has been undermined in any form is that child!"

The human dynamics for cognitive balance is a process that is initiated from home, and then transferred to the society. However, when a child is being let out of the home unchecked, the society does its job without consulting the home. There are conditions at home that we do not realize are avenues for a child to feel that they cannot breathe:

x.   If a child's space at home seems inconvenient, somehow you a pushing him out even without saying it.

x.   If the space is clustered by too many people being around, going outside may be appealing.

x.   If you are too busy and not usually there for your children physically and emotionally to morally support and provide direct care, they are likely to go find it somewhere else, and so on.

After the society had gotten the better part me, I started building a defensive wall as a mechanism to deal with my complexity, fear, vulnerability, and weakness because no one wants to be ridiculed.

The mechanism which was working very well for me was centred on distraction. Distraction was a very good tool for me to put away all those unwanted feelings. It starts with me playing excessively, creating more internal noise in other to block off information, and creating imaginary memories through wishful thinking. This soon degenerated to restlessness, lack of energy and stamina towards learning and practices. I enjoyed procrastination with respect to completing my assignments. I hated the idea of reading and studying. I exhibited a variety of derailing behaviors, which resulted in self-sabotage that evolved in agreement with a mediocre view of me. Of course, I still hate chores and the only reason I'd even done my chores at all was to avoid punishment. In such a case, I attended to it in a haphazard manner just to get myself out of trouble and have more time for play.

Thus, many activities suffered from my being impatient and having less stamina for value adding ventures. I failed examinations because I didn't settle to prepare for them; I lacked self-presentation manners and expression toward others. I quit some dynamic relationships due to shyness; I had an overwhelming feeling of boredom for any structured practice. I lacked confidence, had feelings of unworthiness, emptiness, worthlessness, and adopted anger and bad temper as a response for the slightest provocation, developed bad eating habits, and so on. Most often, I'd hide behind my frowning mask, never wanting to smile or even laugh. I was poorly motivated, and sometimes I felt like running away from my own body. As an adult with the same diagnosed attitude I missed business opportunities by dismissing potential ideas. I kept off negotiations or speaking up for myself because I lost my voice when I lost my confidence. When I "lost my voice", as a coping mechanism, I became a talkative. I didn't even listen to myself when I talked, let alone listening to others. Listening is a virtue and the best form of learning; the best part of communication. It takes patience to master listening but patience was not my thing. When I "lost my voice," I let people negotiate for me on their own terms and thereafter I will complain and suffer. A lot of times, the only option left for me was to let go, and then I see myself back to level zero.

Failure is a demon created by oneself and for them. It has to be conceded that failure is an inevitable occurrence in our everyday endeavours. However, it's a choice; a choice we have made for ourselves when we did not prepare enough. It is possible to let the spirit of failure possess you due to fear, instead of learning from past failures. No one is supposed to live a life undermined by their failures and fears; but the funny thing is, we always have reason or something or someone to blame for our failures and in so doing we stay down.I guess it is a safe place; we cover our shame so as not to be ridiculed. Yet, some of all these habits and behaviors that I have mentioned still exist in us. Some can't even keep relationships; they don't know how to be responsible for anyone else, all because they lack self-respect. In totality, it is powerlessness. I had made myself too small, very small; '*Small Me*' is what I call it.

But irrespective of all these, I had a mental consciousness that I wanted to become successful; I'd wanted a success story, an overcomer's story. I wanted to be very rich and be able to buy myself everything I'll ever want. Not having extra-rich parents that will leave me a share in their estate meant I had to start thinking of different approaches because my wishful thinking can't present that kind of life to me in reality. Self-awareness and self-realization cum re-negotiating with myself on how to bring about the change needed for the better '*Me*' is what this book is about. The desired change is possible only through finding my leadership genius.

Finding leadership is growing, maturing and taking responsibility. This involves the conscious effort of listening to conscience, and discerning the difference between *'what feels good'* and *'what is right for me'*. Knowing that what feels good is the voice of my small me but what is right is the voice of my better me which is my *'Big Me.'*

Hence, *'Small Me'*, *'Big Me'* is a concept of leadership dynamics of a personal journey of leading one's self from nothing to a place of success and pride. This won't be possible without empathy and considerations of both the *'Small Me'* and *'Big Me.'*

'Small Me' was a desperate child who needed to survive when external pressure forced him to slide into safety, which became his comfort zone. For so long he remained in that corner of fear and desperation. Obedience and conformity was the right switch to turn on the safe mode, which had kept him very limited. But realization from the time past has ignited the flint stone of his potential, and rekindled it with oxygen of passion to succeed. His burning desire right now is about leaving the comfort zone, which is now increasingly uncomfortable because the self has started adjusting its size to become suitable for attainment of his place of pride, and surely the needed passion is available. The essence of the burning flint-energy and passion is to stir the internal repre-

sentation; like in combustion, stirring causes expansion, which will result in the appearance of the '*Big Me*'.

Every person has in themselves a basic form of dual personalities contending with each other on every arising matter. In my case, I call my dual persona my '*Big Me*' and '*Small Me*.' So let's get into this journey together in other to indulge you more about my persona's discovery, which is more like finding a flint stone lying potentially under the earth. We will learn how they are sparked to life and eventually became a flame of fire full of energy. The gap between my '*Small Me*' and '*Big Me*' persona is attributed to the level of energy consumed and burnt in the drive to engage or utilise the leadership genius. As we will understand in future, leadership dynamism relates to the burning energy; the higher the energy, the bigger 'The Me' while the lower the energy, the smaller 'The Me.' Our decision making governs the level of energy we harness and it's a continuum. The higher the energy, the more successful we are likely to be, and the lower the energy, the more difficulty we are likely to face. In most cases of low energy, it makes one a victim of circumstance and victims are always under subjection and powerless. In contrast, leaders are not subjected rather objective to symbolized intention fuelled by an induced vision. My '*Big Me*' is a product of determination, self-realization from the time past, a personal search within the accumulation of past experiences, adaptability and self-discipline.

2

'BIG ME; SMALL ME'

...beginning of my leadership journey.

A number of years ago in my dream, I was sitting alone on a pavement by the corner of a narrow street, observing an empty world, with my arms crossed over my chest. Then I saw a horse-wagon approaching slowly towards my direction. I wasn't mindful at first because I didn't expect what was coming. The gentleman in the wagon was modestly dressed in a white silky long blameless tunic. He called out and beckoned on me, disturbing my serene moment of '*Me*' wallowing in the dungeon of self-pity...excitedly and with no hesitation I quickly jumped on his wagon as we rode off along the aisle of green field outside of the city's wall. Then just like a veil off my eyes, that initial frenzy of familiarity disappeared and I realized that I'd joined a stranger I didn't know anything about, how foolish of me! Interestingly, it seemed the stranger was also feeling the same way as I was feeling. A conversation therefore ensued in a manner as though I was being interrogated:

"Do you know who I am?" He asked.

"Of course, I do," trying to hold out a pretentious proffer of familiarity.

"Who am I, to you?" now personalizing his enquiry.

I gazed on his face, in his bright eyes was a fierceness of light that illuminates an appeal for wisdom; it felt like a beam of tiny laser of accentuation. I was perplexed, and at the same moment overwhelmed with timidity. I tried to speak but words were not forth coming. On his stern cheek was a gleam of fainted grin at my discomfort. There was something about his composure that gave out a sense of boldness, bravery, and fearlessness as he communicated with his clear and perfect pitched voice. To cut the long story short, I admitted not knowing him but to my surprise he didn't appear disappointed, rather he admonished me. "Get to know me," he said and then smiled, "you will be glad you did. I know you can be much bigger and better than you are now, it's about finding the bigger version of you." In a wisp of moment, he disappeared leaving me alone in the wagon but I could still hear his coax rolling voice in my head like it was in a distance, "Remember, you must find me!!". Suddenly, I awoke. Considering how real the encounter was, I knew that was the beginning of my leadership journey.

Leadership begins with me. It's a journey of self-realization. When you realize that leadership begins with you and take the first step of accepting and envisioning this reality, then it will be easier for you to navigate through your journey. The obvious is that what you see for yourself creates your perception; that image on the mirror is the me who is desperately in need of growth and change because life has bullied me long enough. I started looking for change and began rephrasing the kind of questions I put out there even in the midst of my wallow. All what I'd achieved so far was the small version of me called '*Small Me*.'

He's a fraternity of all my initial personalities or basically childish characters. This idea construed the needed adaptable measures for growth into the bigger version of me, which is my '*Big Me*'.

Both individualities are the embodiment of who I am as a person; it's the identity of '*My Me*' concept. The identity of '*My Me*' concept seems the same as self-concept but different in the sense that it's about me as the subject and object of the whole narrative. It refers to some of those experiences one has indulged in our past behaviors, beliefs we hold in the present and even future anticipations. They are characteristics we presume to have defined us as who we are; our identity. In this identity context, I have managed to grade them based on their effect on my self-preservation. We act based on these factors of influence: external influence and internal representation.

An external influence in social psychology proves that exposure of ourselves to external matters influences the way we react. The external factor explains how people around us make us feel and act.

The internal representation is based on how we perceive and process the information we obtained. Some are in quick response, while some are carefully thought out, which maybe our final decision. This explains how we deal with information and any decision is either good for me or right for me. For clarity, there is nothing like a bad decision, but the outcomes of your actions are what people make reference towards.

'*Big Me*' and '*Small Me*' were well crafted as a concept that will enable my *ME*s' function side by side; each of my *Me* have their turns based on the situation but not without dialogue in my head - that's the mentality check.

'*Big Me*' as the grown up or mature aspect of Me exhibit qualities like empathy, '*what is right aspect*', and selflessness. He's the person I want to become with continuous learning and improvement. The '*Small Me*' is the growing part of me, with qualities like sympathy, '*what is good aspect*', and egocentricity; that's the person I'm now.

This concept will help us explain our mindset and it is important to know that we are all having internal conversation at all times but maybe some of us are not aware of it. Our actions are played out on the side of the more domineering voice and those voices are non-stop on differing issues, for instance, when my internal voice of responsibility, usually my '*Big Me*'s voice keeps dominating, then he's on the verge of taking responsibility as ideologically he's got the voice of a leader, emotional awareness, and self-awareness. But then on the contrary, if my "*Small Me's* voice dominates, then all my actions will be based on a follower's ideology; active or in some cases passive.

Let's look at this funny narrative of mine; I love beer, sometimes I close my eyes and imagine me in a bar with other drinking buddies, in a camaraderie unison proclaiming our love... "We, the people of Greenfield mother nature hereby declare our love for you, Beer!" We love the smooth and thirst quenching feeling of triple filtered brewed barley grain extract... that's what we stand for!!! "So drink up ladies and gentlemen!" In a loud and vehement expression, the crowd cheers!!!...I'm actually laughing at myself while I'm writing this because I can feel my '*Small Me*' saying "Hallelujah!"

But in all honesty, whenever you meet any drunken person, and ask, "It seems you are drunk already?" He'll never agree to be under any influence...drunk people always and vehemently refutes the obvious... "No, I'm not drunk, don't say that!" It's funny to hear or see a drunk in his denial, even with his feeble knees and staggering motion. Alcoholism and drug abuse in general are depressants and they are not necessarily what we think it is for us... An escape! I am not in any way trying to derogate anybody in their choice of alcohol in-take but a narrative built on its excesses as a form of self-distraction.

This could be characteristic of the 'Small Me'; unaware of my immediate surroundings, unaware of himself, in some cases unconscious and without levelled faculty. This is the same feeling some people have all their lives; being unaware, not stepping up when it comes to reasoning, in constant denial of their state and faculty imbalance, in constant denial of their faults, in constant denial that they can amount to anything if they make conscious effort to change. They don't believe in the possibility of their ability to change their situation; in constant denial that this life is worth living, thereby becoming suicidal and a possible danger to themselves and to the society.

Self-awareness is the conscious effort one makes in other to understand one's own self further by searching inwardly in other to balance personal values and standards against his current behavioral pattern. Self-awareness is attained by process of continuous self-evaluation and consideration of factors that brings about change, growth, and adaptability. '*Small Me*' maybe laughing earlier but there is a record high on my responsibility scale, which shows that my self-control and self-discipline is at its highest. This further fuels my commitment to complete the writing of this book. I am persuaded that I'm more deliberate with my actions than ever before. There is a mentality scale that weighs between the '*Big Me*' and the '*Small Me*'; the scale measures every shift in mentality between them. If success and growth is an obligation, to become responsible and to invest in one's self is inevitable.

When one understands one's self and decides to grow and to become a success, he will devise a vivid means of intrapersonal dialogue between the two uncompromising personalities in his head like my *MEs*. It also can be referred as identity, which are those characteristics that an individual thinks defines them. '*Big Me*' and '*Small Me*' are sitting on the conscientious scale as seen in below diagrams weighing heavy to bend every action and conversation to their own favor.

Dual persona on the scale of conscience:

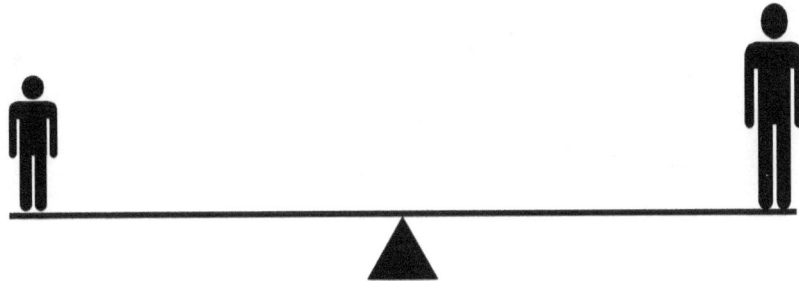

(Fig 2.1- 'Big Me' and 'Small Me' on the balance)

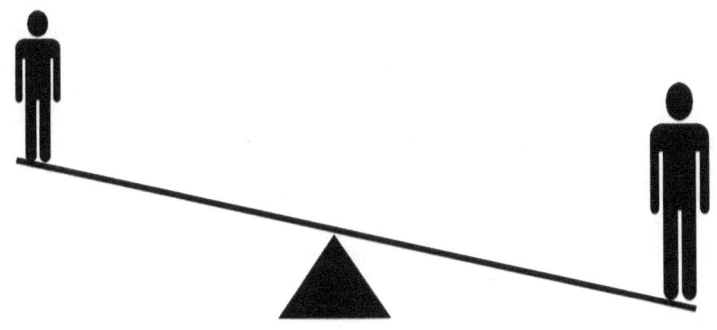

(Fig 2.2-*'Big Me'* weighing down-'what is right')

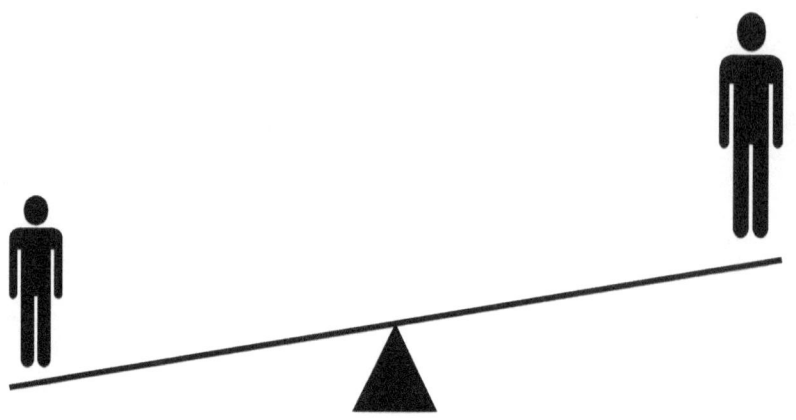

(Fig 2.3-'*Small Me*' weighing down-'what is good.')

When situations are presented, the decision to call on is "how do you respond?" and this determines who will win. But sometimes, situations can shift and it might warrant change of mind. I feel some of my readers are already perceiving a part of me '*Small Me*' with a bias all thanks to its poor mentality but that is not completely what it is in this case. The '*Big Me*' and '*Small Me*' is the ambivalence persona, described effortlessly as the person '*I am*' now and the person '*I am*' aspiring to become respectively. The person '*I am*' now is never satisfied with himself whereas the person I want to become is continually beckoning on me to come up, and that is the real journey of leadership. For some people, their present state is comfortable enough; that's their comfort zone, and that is why it may seem impossible for them to make up their minds. Yet, starting on your success journey, one needs to be aware of challenges that must be surmounted, which are embedded in the place of decision making. The decision to start, the decision to quit, the decision to persevere, the decision to change, the decision to decide, and so on.

Decision making is based on our negotiation between one's head and heart. When the brain and mind disagrees as they often do, there are always moments of pause and play. The issue about disagreement can never be over emphasized as we are constantly at it with ourselves and with others. Actions to decide, deciding actions, and action after decision all points to the importance of decision making. Decision making in this perspective are broadened into two parallel flows; *good decisions* and *right decisions* as will align in our context. Right decision may show no immediate impart or result but maybe best for long time goals, whereas good decisions are ones for a short time goal. Good decisions could be for quick fixes, immediate relief, which may even involve tampering with the basic universal principle.

Every right minded person avoids making important decisions in hurry whether it is rational or irrational. Most times, people wrestle between what I will call *good decision* and *right decision* because they are sure it is not breaking the law but the effect in the long run must be considered. Whenever a decision is unanimously reached, which is both right and good, balance is achieved, and it is called Homogeneity. You will know who is deciding in either of the two based on the action; depending on if it is for selfish, egocentric reasons or for the betterment of everyone. Breaking limits on personal growth usually requires taking decisions that are for general well-being and organizational growth.

If a leader is deciding or making decisions based on his imbalance scale, the tendency of his lapses will be very eminent. If the decision is just the right choices, then immediate challenges may suffer and vice versa. The best is to take decisions in a timely manner on the balance scale to deal with both ends; this usually gives a sense of actualization. Self-actualization is clearly the process of growth and leading one's self a step forward at a time. There are high chances that if you don't persevere, you would lag behind. Picking up resilience is a Thor hammer, because there is a thin line between an achiever and a mediocre. If you understand leadership dynamics you will know and understand your place in order to bring out the best in you at all times. There will be mistakes and more mistakes, but what matters is keeping tabs, and being accountable. Self-actualization is simply hedging one's success in order to get some more success. Actualization for a leader is a hunger for more success and not the end of the road. Fulfilling a course should stir up another course.

The term self-fulfilled sounds to me as arrogance and motivation at the same time; it is reserved for actually sparking a passion for motion for more achievement. To be fulfilled requires balance. If I let my '*Big Me*' and '*Small Me*' in, then we should remember that the journey from '*Small Me*' to '*Big Me*' should unify like a journey from a level to another level. The rungs of a ladder will help us to understand this concept, assume '*Small Me*' to be the lowest rung and '*Big Me*' to be the next upper rung. Actualization can happen if there is desire. This desire can be assumed as a push force and success is attained by successfully pushing '*Small Me*' up to the next upper rung... so if you attain success, and have no desire to pursue another, then you are likely to remain small on that level as there is always a higher rung.

3

LEADERSHIP

"Leadership is the most valuable commodity but the rarest commodity we have…"

Bob Davids

"We are all witnesses on a daily basis of how through uncompromising drift the world and the system is moving towards virtuality…"

Edu Darlington

Leadership has an unending reel of definitions from different authors and people. Everyone has tried to their own best ability to explain its content as conceptual as they could; yet, I believe that leadership is everything and in everything; it is 'Omni'. Leadership is everywhere and in everything. It just depends on what and how you represent it to be for you. For me, I stand firmly on the view that it is energy and responsibility. Energy when it comes to our mind-driven world and responsibility when it is about work or physical driven contents. In other sense, thinking of it (ideas) and getting it to work (application). Leadership is creativity, a learn-able skill set or talent in the sense of a gift one can improve on. The discipline to apply it can be learnt through a humility model of serving without ego. In so many ways, I think leadership is first-ly subconscious.

The extent of innovations and technology in our world today pro-vides signs of the subconscious coming to reality. These innova-tions are seriously driving our world through its unprecedented solutions. Innovators like Zuckerberg with his leading role in building the Facebook platform to connect the world, and Steven Jobs who modelled a box and interface so slick like apple laptop, IPad, and IPod thus making the computer system user friendly and in every home, are thinking leaders with a keen sense for change. Even in the recent times, innovations from Tesla, apps, google, and so on, are pushing boundaries beyond our common imagination in the area of intelligence and communication in our world, thereby creating more visibility in the dynamism of our leadership. These are but a few demonstration of our point; lead-ership has since moved from a place of nobility to the place of radicals in mind. Your dignity is worthless if you're not creative. A simple evidence is the shift from the era of slavery (servitude) to-wards mechanization and industrialization. Now we are living in the era of automation and I.T, innovation, artificial intelligence, robotics, and many other countless to come.

Unfortunately, most of us are still glued on the leadership of the "old" and do not want to appreciate the leadership of the "now"; and that narrows it down to just "followers and leaders", instead of "vision of leaders and active followers", which is the future. The future is bright for every creative mind because artificial intelligence, machine learning through algorithm and robots are here to stay. I'm obliged to quench the immediate thirst for archaism, because even if the future is unknown to us, should we stay put and grow extinct or better still become irrelevant? That's food for thought, and the question remains what will be your position?

Leadership position; Leadership position is a sense of superiority adopted by an individual among his peers by the virtue of their odds. When one obtains certain qualities that give them advantages over another or others, they tends to take lead over his peers. Such qualities include physical strength (which may be considered outdated), been more skillful or talented in a certain relevant act, richer than others (monetary or material resources), and physical appearance like beauty. These sorts of advantages apply as long as the odds don't change. That is why it is important that everyone should update and upgrade their statue and standards. What great leaders do is to learn and re-learn so as to be able to be ahead of others or eventful challenges. Our world keeps evolving and the old ways are steadily phasing out while the new ways are quietly sliding in and taking over, and the slide needs adaptable **leaders'** not archaic nobles. Adaptable leaders are leaders who constantly evolve and believe in change. They believe in doing everything possible to stay in the flow of change. They also have the ability of influencing others to become leaders, knowing that the world needs more leaders, as there is a scarcity and dire need for leaders and leadership.

Leadership development; Leadership development now has pre-eminence beyond organizational ladders as this present world with abundance of information entails that old ways of doing things become extinct. Development exists in every corner and in view of keen minds much more than ever before. Individuals are going out of their ways to learn new things every day, in other to acquire an edge of advantage to be able to compete in this our continuously evolving world. Leadership development is like a rotating cogwheel attached to another rotating cogwheel, the system might start rough but the more the adjustments, the smoother and faster the speed of the rotation. In some cases, the cogwheel will be combined with another cogwheel using a belt to form a pulley for moving up an item; that is purpose found. Leadership development is purpose driven. The purpose is to have leaders in every possible level, whose jobs are to teach and develop more leaders, because organizations and societies that **win** are cogwheel strategic, anchoring on a consistent and practical coaching, training and practicing. Cogwheel strategy of leadership is implemented successfully via:

1. Experience.
2. Creating coach-able principles based on sound strategy of operations in business and in society in general.
3. Insight into significance of values (culture) in the workplace.
4. Conducive workplace and positive emotional energy.
5. Calling for, and supporting right decision making.
6. Motivation.

Development could also be considered same as growth… "a tree doesn't make a forest." For any leader to succeed he must be ready to develop others in other to form hedges around themselves for defence and assured succession.

Leadership approach; This aspect of leadership is very important because leaderships' approach in its dealings usually goes in a way not everyone understands. This will help us learn how to deal with others. However, before I'll proceed, let me highlight an important virtue of a leader, which is emotional intelligence. Emotional intelligence is an important skill any leader should have as it deals with empathy. We will dwell more on it in chapter 6. Leadership approach can be patterned towards a transformational approach or transactional approach. Robert Kiyosaki stated in his book "8 Lessons in Military Leadership, 2015." that all great leaders are sales people, and of course that is true. Therefore, if developing leaders is important at all levels in any organization as we have seen earlier, then it is important that we should be aware of our pattern of approach.

Transactional approach expresses a leader's tyrannical propensity with little or no empathy. It's about using an irrational model, which negatively affects the whole culture of a group making the members not to be empathic to one another and even to people outside the group. For organizations, there are in-group (internal) and out-group (external) exchanges. Every single exchange requires a certain department in the organization to handle them; for instance; sales, accounting, marketing, debt collection, etc. The way customers are treated is a reflection of the organization's leadership and the calibre of their emerging leaders.

I had an experience with a certain subscription company. At a time my home internet network subscription was due and I was defaulting in my payment. Soon, I started getting calls from the provider concerning the bill. On one of these occasions, I got a call from one of their male sales representatives. I was trying to assure him that I will surely pay off as soon as I could; I was explaining that I was having some issues with a cheque at the time, but this guy who is unknown to me started yelling, ranting and threatening me with a lawsuit and police. I simply hung up on him, then he tried to ring me back but I didn't take his calls and eventually stopped picking calls from the company.

However, days later, I courageously took my last call from one of their representatives, this time it was a lady. I asked her to simply use my security deposit to reimburse my outstanding and register my account for disconnection. She tried to dissuade me, but I had already made up my mind. That is one client lost to their competitor. Of course, in some cases, debts maybe long overdue and debt recovery may need a little push but empathy must be shown. Debt collectors are more like sales people but in this case in reverse, for bad credit. All in all, their job description must not be unbearable for clients as this may have unfavourable outcomes for the organization.

At another time, I was 3 weeks behind in my rent payment; my landlord called me and asked if there is any way he could help. I simply asked for more time, which he obliged, and it didn't take me long to pay him back in full. It is important to note that he had given me more time and less hassle, thereby allowing me to deal with my issue as soon as possible and pay up with little or no stress. Sales people are good in luring people to their product and services but are usually not good in helping them to deal with their debt. It's important to point out that a good number of debtors are defaulting due to unfortunate incidents that may have occurred to disrupt their earning process; for instance, loss of job, loss of business, failed attempts on new businesses, credit mismanagement, and so on. In whatever way the issue of debt surfaces, companies must handle it in a business-like manner with empathy and not as a wrong doing or crime. Corporate organizations must be consistent in their dealing with clients irrespective of whether it is during sales or during debt recovery.

Transformational approach describes a leader's motives and operation with empathy; the approach thrives in giving to the people first, helping out, and serving with transparency and no selfish interest. The approach is always a win-win situation where your client remains loyal in future dealings. Transformational leadership approach in our society begins with absolutely identifying and recognizing the rights of the most vulnerable in the group, be it the women, the children, the old and more importantly our environment. In some part of the world, especially in Africa, cultural practices recommends that children are supposed to honour their elders by basically giving up their rights and in so doing the elderly will now be able to love back as a compensation.

In our society, all segments of people must be honoured ranging from children to adults. Honoring children is by keeping their dignity intact and self-esteem high. Any form of child abuse and child labor is a dishonoring act on the child. Physical beatings and punishment just to bend them to conform to your will is not acceptable. Violence, domestic violence against women or even anybody, and neglect of the elderly is not acceptable.

Considering the big picture, if the future of our offspring is so important to us, why don't we also start considering the earth we are all living in? Climate change is not a hoax. Although the earth has a way of replenishing itself, it is not catching up with the rate at which we are degrading her. We may not be able to stop natural disasters, but if the generation to come must have a home, then we must protect our world from pollution; such as plastic dumps in our oceans, harmful chemicals discharge to the eco and aquatic system, wildfires, and fuel emissions. So leadership should be proactive and futuristic in thinking. It must also be stated that we all have a part to play; with everyone's contribution helping to keep us all safe, we honor our children and protect our world.

Leadership power and empowerment; A leader cannot obtain power except when given to him by his followers, and only then can he empower others. That's exactly how Bob Davids best describes it in his words; "when the people you're leading gives you their support (like power), they have offered you power and they watch you… if you take that power and reflect all of it back to them, then they will give you more, and if you take it and give all of it back the second time to them, they will give you back even more. But if you hold back some of that power, they will start giving you less…so many leaders today failed because they took the power and did not give it back to the people they are leading… leadership is a gift. You can't buy nor sell it, you can't trade it, you either have it or you don't…" This is similar to the second law of thermodynamics, "Energy can neither be created nor destroyed but can be transformed from one form to another." Bob's narrative reveal that power is something obtainable in the shift dynamic of objectiveness by being more transformational in getting people to respond to your desired way, this is called emotional competence. Emotional competence makes a demand on a leader to lead by example in all endeavors toward his followers. Leaders are first empowered, and then they can empower their followers.

Follower-ship; The lens for most to view and understand leadership is through the follower's point of view. If there is nobody following, then no one is leading. The position of who comes first between leadership and follower-ship is certainly unknown as both cannot be separated and I do not have evidence to support any of the views. There is always impertinence towards follower-ship that makes it seem as though irrelevant, but only a leader will be able to explain the importance of followers. Leadership and follower-ship have stood side by side through all times, and evolved through the ages. I'm yet to come across any other practice couple that has the same height of adaptability. Followers are the real mirror images of a leader. When they are happy the leader is happy; when they are complaining, definitely there is trouble in the paradise. Anyways, a mirror is a subjective image representation of a person or an object. Whatever image you closely recognize has a message for you; a call to decipher. Followers are the reflection of their leaders, whatever the leadership approach; be it transactional or transformational.

4

RAISING A LEADER

"Leadership is a unique talent that needs to be nurtured, and it's some-thing everyone has in them, no exception."

John Maxwell.

"Train up a child in the way he should go; and when he is old, he will not depart from it."

Proverb 22:6.

Mary and Jane were single mothers and each of them had a tod-dler son. Both ladies liked to burn fancy fragrant candles when-ever they were home, especially during evening periods. Jane would light her candle and places it on the centre table in the living room and her little boy always crawls and struggles to touch the fascinating candle flame. Her son's efforts usually draws her attention while preparing dinner, because she has to keep taking him away from burning flame of the candle. On the other hand, Mary would light up her candle and hangs it high on the wall to avoid her son reaching the burning candle. She does her dinner preparation without having to worry about her son getting hurt by the candle flame even when she sees him struggling to reach for the candle.

One day, an older lady who frequently visits both young ladies went over to Jane's apartment. She noticed that Jane's son was approaching the burning candle, her motherly instinct kicked in and she made it straight to stop him. "Let him! Leave him to touch it, so he can learn a good lesson that flames or fire can burn" said Jane who had grown weary of having to stop him from going for the burning candle. The older lady did as she ordered, and Jane's little boy learnt his first lesson with fire. The older woman then asked her why... "I did it so that in his life he will keep away from danger, fire and whatever out there that has the tendency to hurt him"

The next day, the same lady went over to Mary's apartment and wondered...then she enquired of her on why she puts her candle on a holder high off the wall. Mary answered, "Firstly, it's beautiful up on the wall. Secondly, because of my son who tries to reach up to the burning candle all the time; I don't want him to get hurt, because it might ruin his chances due to fear. If he continues reaching up to the candle light, it might help increase his sense of curiosity and adventure; besides, I can prepare dinner without having to worry about him."

In the above narrative, between these two single mothers, who do you think is raising her own baby better? I will let you be the judge ...

Parenting is an act of bravery and a very tedious job because every aspect of it has to be deliberate for a given purpose. The practice of parenting is a natural process that sets out the initial trajectory of human dynamism and discipline influenced by the ideology and belief of the parents. It births who a child will become in the future through character emulation and resemblance. I concede that other factors such as genetic order and environment also contributes to who a child becomes. The natural phenomena of character and attitude are formed as a result of development via instinct and behavioral replication. However, every child has their own uniqueness; even children of the same parents are different, even in the case of identical twins. The uniqueness of a child always manifest in the demonstration of their ability in a particular task. Genetic ability, which is the intelligence influenced by the gene and environment proves a child's uniqueness in form of talents and skills. These can be harnessed and honed in the process of child's development.

Child development is an embodiment of a child's growth and advancement, which follows from how a child is raised. Parenting as we have seen is practically nurturing whereas raising is about building up the child. It has to be intentional for survival and adaptation. The idea is simply to raise a child that will lead; it is like a common assignment and competition among all parents to raise a child that will always be at the fore front. The way a child is raised has a lot to do with their ability to tap more into their genetic ability. Every perceived information will be internalized, compartmented as memories, and referenced to whenever a new challenge surfaces. If the most stored information in their memories are based on bravery, courage and positivity, the tendency that their responses will always come from a positive mental attitude will be eminent, and vice versa. I want to believe most parents would want to self-commend their effort at the end of having been able to raise a leading child.

...If that is utterly true, I'm left to believe that Jane's style of parenting of infusing pain and fear may inhibit his son from learning new things, while Mary's approach might be right and better in safe guarding her baby's sense of curiosity.

Children are supposed to be curious and curiosity is a dynamic strength that positions children to become thinkers, thereby having the ability to question everything around them. The place of curiosity is where their understanding and realization is formed. It the realization of who they really are with pride as should a leader. This sense of pride gives them an edge or advantage in their performance. When an advantage keeps yielding positive leads for a child that makes the difference for a leading child. The difference between a lead child and non-lead child is not just about early traits found in child like unruly swift physical development, prodigy, self-confidence, and extraversion, but it's about gradual cognitive development, mental balancing, and strengthened physical capability. Therefore, the ability of a child to mutate and respond to change is key to developing their leadership potential.

Leadership is more of a creation from a child's uniqueness and experience through discovery. Take for instance, stones have always had potential even while lying around everywhere, but it was not until the discovery of its ability to start fires that its true worth came to fore. I hope this will help answer a long standing enquiry whether a leader is born or made. John Maxwell said "I have never seen an unborn leader..." Therefore, there is a leadership potential in everyone/child like a flint stone. It's a creation to be discovered. This gem in a child has to push dynamically in other to position a child's mental ability beyond the limitations of the parenting they received. These limitations are as we may understand can be due to;

x   Parental limited belief/ illiteracy /ignorance/lack of understanding and exposure.

x   Occurrence and constant change in some practices in our society, for example, technological innovation.

x   Preventing a child from expressing themselves and non-acceptance of a child's best ability due to genuine instinct of protecting the child from emotional and physical harm.

x   Overly and high parental expectations from a child.

So, parenting is simply nurturing a child but creation through training/education is what raises or grooms a leader. Both can happen simultaneously in preparing a leader. Grooming a leader has two factors that influences its process; intelligence and environmental.

Intelligence factor; Every child is born with a genius that distinguishes him, which is to say that intelligence factor could be dubbed differently in every one. This factor shines light on human dynamics, as the collective applied efforts and discipline undergo by a person or child in achieving continuous set goal.

Also, intelligence factor can be referred as human dynamic quotient. It is a collation of data on a timely basis in other to substantiate development in a child. Obtained data can be formal or informal, and it is useful to predict expectation of a child in the future. Formal collation is in print in form of records for future referencing whereas informal is an optimistic approach in a sense that development of a child may not have a vivid record storage but effective and impressive notable knowledge. For example, health record of a child is a formal print while talent has no objective form of record for grading, rather a sketchy comparison may be dubbed.

Human dynamic quotient foils out mediocrity and other agents in a lead-child's performance that would have probable cause in deterring the expectation of a developing child. It is important for designing and designating strategically practices in other for a superior mental development to be achieved. And superior mental development gives a child a flawless wit, and intelligence that is required in other for any child to properly get in touch with their genius.

Environmental factor: The factor embraced human dynamics in a wider spectrum in developing a lead-child or a leader. Child's development is a process that deals with interaction between a child and the society. It is a continuous process of negotiating identities and shaping one's self concept, various attitudes and behaviors of the individual as related by (Strykes; 1979)

Prior to every other external interaction, home is the first place of learning for every developing child or children. It presents a child with comfort and safety, but may deprive him an opportunity of being exposed to the wider surrounding. This initial non-exposure may prove difficult to deal with as the child may be lagging in development of instinct and adaptation for survival. But this can be remedied through caregivers and parents who have understanding of these concepts helping the affected children initiate positive shifts in their behavioral pattern. Behavioral pattern of every child differs as a result of the kind of environment they are exposed to; environmental variables could be positive or negative.

Positive environmental variables present situations that are fair in support of a child's development, for example, peaceful environment with orderliness that supports good education, sufficient supply of basic resources like nutritious food, healthcare and so on. On the contrary, negative variables present situations that are unfair, which doesn't support proper development of a child or children. For example, war time in a zone would never give education room to thrive, pandemic like the Corona virus spree. Those children in an area with poor or no internet connection, or who their parents cannot afford the internet costs won't be able to get provided online education. Other negative variables may include environmental pollution, child-abuse, poverty, neglect, inconsistent expectation, and child's deprivation and so on. All these variables, both positive and negative shape a child's attitude and perception.

An individual's attitude is evaluated with respect to a target. Target could be objective or subjective. Attitude can be evaluated as a measure of how appreciative or non-appreciative a person is. 'Alive (social psychology-(2006)) by Breckler, Olson and Wiggins. Perception as the ability for a person, child or adult, to see, hear, smell, taste and feel. The sensory receptors of a child are constantly at work due to their curiosity, and every information consumed is classified as pleasurable or painful, thereby forming an internal representation for response. Those are the major cognitive approach for their learning ability.

Remember earlier, when my 'Small Me' was in charge, he did justice to bad feeling by fending it off but when the feeling seem to persist; he started building a defence for safety. The same may be the case for some other children out there going through difficulty, which they may not understand. They will build a tall wall and threshold of defence around themselves in order to survive. The elevated wall may cause the following; self-sabotage as they find a means of distraction (self-distraction), loss of voice as they keep mute instead of speaking up, loss of confidence, and shying away from engagements. Imminent danger and fear of the unknown created a smaller version of me and same can reduce any child instead of build them. Our aim is to learn how to build up children and raise leaders.

The world is in dire need of leadership and the job of every adult or caregiver should be to provide an enabling environment so that children can have the best chance of developing responsibly. To raise a lead-child requires continuously encouraging that child to internalize positive mental attitudes through a clear developmental program such as coaching.

5

LEADERSHIP STRATEGY

"Vision is the principal thing…"

" …who can tell me, what is the first thing or the most important quality for coaching?" standing patiently, smiling, as most of us were yelling different inappropriate answers. "Vision! my dear friends" said The Boss, answering his own question. "Without vision, it is unlikely for anyone to make it as a coach. A coach can be a mentor, an influencer, a leader, a motivator, a teacher, whatever that suits you…"

We cannot talk about strategy without understanding vision. Vision goes beyond the superficial, and holds strong on the carrier. Vision is simply the ability to observe, to understand the time we are in as viewed from our past, and the situations, which will guide one towards and through future challenges. Challenges can be immediate or in the future. In whatever way we encounter any challenge, the main aim is to sort through it and make sure it is handled correctly. Besides, challenges have been proven to be endless and never ceasing (i.e. coming in different forms); it can also be said that different challenges come with different forms of energy. We all face challenges all the time. Leaders are always meeting with challenges of different magnitudes and prospects. And every level of challenge a leader overcomes will qualify him for a high challenge. Some challenges need an immediate response while some may not. Of course, if it's not an emergency but very important to be tackled, appropriate time can be taken in order to handle it in the best possible way. Some challenges are incessant and keep reoccurring, and it's very important that it's dealt with; a plan may need to be devised in order to completely eradicate it or control or manage it, (e.g. humanity associated challenges like hunger, poverty, security, housing, and so on).

Having vision goes beyond immediate circumstances, but interestingly, vision and strategy is primarily needed in order to handle present challenges. I often hear people say vision is for the future but I think that the future is now...observe, diagnose the problem, and then fix it.

The most realistic and workable plan or procedure for tackling problems is strategy. Strategy is a well-planned action path to achieving victory...victory does not come out by doing nothing or by default. That is not what leaders do, they plan and prepare to win. Strategy entails knowing what to do among many things competing for the better part of our attention. It's the why, and how to get everything done.

Leadership strategy is a process of realistic actions designed in other to continually overcome challenges, for instance, security measures against crimes and criminals. Most leaders are not visionaries, but all leaders must have a vision. Vision is an anchor which directs the dynamism of leadership towards an anticipated and desired outcome. *"Write the vision and make it plain" Habakuk 2:2.*

If a strategy is for winning, the nature of its preparation and development is therefore important. Preparation is everything one has previously put in place in other to achieve a successful outcome; both consciously and unconsciously. Consciously, because you are focusing on the desired outcome or performance and that drives you to practice, train, and study. Unconsciously, because your actions are not prompted by any particular event, however, you are engaging in the actions hoping that an opportunity will present itself in a familiar ground where you previous actions will come in handy. "It is better to be ready and have no opportunity than having opportunity and not ready." said Les Brown. In general terms, at all times, there is an event to attend, to plan, because everything one indulges in is an event.

Now, as a youth soccer coach, my job is to prepare my players every day via training and practices. For reader's clarity, those two words are not the same. Training is a process of teaching, coaching, inspiring someone in a particular subject or drill, but practice is when the learner repeats the subject or drill over and over again in order to become better on it.

Training by coaches prepares players with respect to techniques and tactics, especially youth coaches. We coaches love to see development and improvements in the techniques of every player, because without basic strong technique, it's impossible to implement a tactic successfully. We need players to be able to receive, control and pass effectively, and of course have basic dribbling capability, which is effective footwork control of the ball. Being skillful is a natural phenomenon no one teaches a player, but any player with enough passion is capable and can learn his own style of effective ball control. Tactics is a synergy of techniques and some level of skills and talents from different players in a team. Every team play in a tactical formation inside the field, and however they run with the ball and after the ball, the aim is to get goals and more goals in order for them to win. The games are played by the set rules; every meaningful game comes with rules and regulations that guide it.

For me, match days are most critical of all days. I have learned that youth players are embedded with potentials and different levels of abilities. While some are quick to put their ability to use, some are catching up, while some are behind catching their breath. Your obligation as a coach is to deal with them as a team. And the very lesson there, on the subject of leadership dynamics is that we are all born with different levels of potential. It is our commitment that determines if we will become the leader we are meant to be. It is important to remember that just as winning is very important to your team, it is equally important to the opposing team. Whatever the outcome, one thing that is very important is commending the team for their great effort. Before, during, and after the game, motivation is critical. Motivation is the next level on the ladder of strategy. Churchill understood that aspect better than most people. He would always motivate the British soldiers during WWII in most of his speeches... *"We will fight in the air, we will fight in the sea, if the enemy wants the fight in the mud, so shall we give it to them."*

People's understanding of your vision is the first reason they would want to follow you or engage with you. And the more clearer the vision becomes, might be the reason for them to remain in course till the end. However, challenges along the way may be very daunting and some would want to throw in the towel, because they are getting tired and demotivated. This is where the strategic move of motivation comes in handy. In a practical sense, you need to reiterate to them the reason why they started in the first place and the benefits in staying in the course; repaint for clarity.

Motivation is creating understanding. Motivation on its own is a versatile subject, and it can come in handy at different levels of human needs. According to Mosley's pyramidal sketch, motivation can be helpful in meeting physiological, safety, social, self-esteem, and self-actualization needs. Moseley maintains that motivation creates an internal disruption that can affect our behavioral outcome. Motivation can be broadly viewed in two aspects; intrinsic and extrinsic motivation. Both are important for the vision carrier and the vision helper. Extrinsic motivation usually emanates from a leader to followers, a coach to players, and from a teacher to the student.   However, to reassure people with words is not always easy; you need to reach out to your followers at the very point of their need. Your players always need support, but they can only talk to you about it if they trust you as their coach. Employee motivation can be through; incentives (the way people tip bar tenders), creating a conducive workplace as it makes them happy, and treating them well so that they will treat your clients and customers well. Show your employees kindness in such a way they will learn from you; motivate in a way they really need you. Reward them specially even though this can be deceptive or manipulative... Deception is also strategic paradigm. I often use the captain's band or best player's sentiment to arouse my players into putting more effort, and this works perfectly all the time.

Sometimes, even a leader can also get demotivated due to a number of factors, and they often don't have any one to turn to but themselves. It's important that you remember the reason you started in the first place, the reason you are in what you are doing, and the help it has provided and is providing to the people who have given you their trust. Your intrinsic motivation will always deal with you like my 'Small Me' and 'Big Me' arguing. 'Small Me' will always come up with good reasons to let go but on the contrary, 'Big Me' would always come up with right reasons to have one more go at whatever it is.

'Small Me': "If you're tired, it's ok, I don't mind resting a bit or maybe it isn't worth all this stress and trouble."
'Big Me': "Yeah, it is a tiring job/practice but we've come a long way to quit now; let's give it one more go, you never know..."
'Small Me': "What? I have been here long enough to know what's going to work or not... at least I have been here longer than you."
'Big Me': "I don't want have this argument now. All I'm saying is a little more push and let's see how it goes..."

Strategy works well in a collective unit as tactics, which is why the skill and techniques of a lone player doesn't always win matches. Same with military groups, no single valour soldier wins a war, battle maybe with automatic assorted riffle. Same goes for organizations; no one employee can do everything by himself, it requires support from other members in the organization. Therefore, outcome of every engagement is a responsibility of the leader and then whole team.

If you are dealing with young players, you will understand this aspect better, undesired results are not to be left to the players/kids to deal with. Each time the team has unfavourable results, straightaway I know what to do; I'll switch gears to *'encourage'* them and to restore in them a healthy mindset. In the 2006 movie 'Gridiron Gang', Dwayne 'The rock' Johnson was a typical example; as the head coach to the juvenile team, he reminded them that the outcome of the game doesn't define who they are and he will definitely choose them above any other team… including the opponent team that just got them down. Such assurance is heavenly. If possible, take all the blame in other to avoid any situation where team members get into fights with one another for any mistake or mistakes which occurred that cost them the game.

In fact, if my team loses a match, I often take the blame because I should have given them a better tactics of play. That is what leaders do; bear or take responsibility for the loss. Coach Mehran, Senior coach and Director of Alliance Football Academy will always ask his team after every game to "take a deep breath for a moment and just think about the good side of the game, and also think about what they will improve in their next game with respect to tactics and techniques. Because at the end of the day, what really matters is that they came out to have fun, and most importantly to learn." A lot of coaches are known for their ego but in some moments, we need to swallow our pride and speak to players with in a good spirit.

Another level of strategy is deception. We have mentioned it earlier. It is clearly in a word defined as "stratagem" and it is basically to trick or lure your opponent on the field into giving up an advantage, in other for your team to win; it is what tactics is all about in the game. Coaches are in no place to negotiate winnings for his team off the pitch with the other team, it's against the ethics of the game. It's either you win or your opponent does. For instance, in the game of football, the "counter attack" tactic of play is one of those tricks; you lure your opponent team into your own half of the pitch, and then seek the opportunity to run ahead of them to score against them. But in the organization and society, deception can always find you out. So most often, negotiation is the best option in resolving issues, and the best negotiation is always to provide a level ground where there is a win-win situation for every party rather than a win-loss situation. But if the parties involved refuse to engage, then every party is left with a loss-loss situation. In such cases, the more daring organization may look for a loophole to take advantage of the other in order to get a win.

The vision of a sports coach may differ from that of a societal leader, but desired outcomes are the same. Every game we play is different from the last, irrespective of whether you won or lost. Likewise, the challenges faced by leaders in the society are always different. My vision as a coach is to help every youth or young player that I come across with to develop into a better person for the sake of humanity. My strategy is to proactively getting them prepared for imminent opportunities ahead. Writing this book seems like part of the plan to be able to push forward the fulfillment of my vision. Desired outcomes come after effective preparations while unsuccessful or undesired outcomes can be fallout of ineffective preparation. Other factors can come into play and lead to undesirable results but in a case where nothing intrusive happens, then my statement becomes more valid.

In football, players train continually, sometimes every day in order to attain highest technique levels, perfect team tactics, and keep up fitness and stamina. But what happens or why do team sometimes lose, even when they have prepared adequately? The reasons are simple, the opponent team were more strategic in applying their tactics.

Maybe other unfavorable factors like drop in stamina, weather condition such as direction of sunlight, fatigue from commuting, internal team conflict, and presence of a higher and experience and technique player in the opposing team. The list can go on but excuses do not produce winners. During games, there could be magical moments that could also turn things around, if a player is able to connect or anchor those moments, it is a prowess and a plus. That's why when preparing, they should be presence of professionalism and absence of mediocrity.

Some young people can be more like the '*Small Me*' all the time. But aspiring players who feel like their life depends on every game, burns their boat and practice with every fibre inside of their being, and on each match day, plays their hearts out.

In concluding this chapter, every good leader has one thing in common; vision. It's a driving force, but having vision alone can't make one stand out among others except with strategy. Strategy brings vision to reality. Strategy is put in action during planning and execution; this is where one is distinguished from others. Sometimes things can jump over board and beyond borders; when the vision is clear, it requires that a leader should be able to pursue through rather than quitting. For a leader to keep up with the expanse of his vision, they should be able to acquire more information as it is necessary. Any prized information acquired is called Intel. Intel I believe it is the abbreviation for intelligence, and most effective strategy of a leader is supposed to have leadership intelligence.

6

Leadership intelligence

*...it's a quest between boarders of uncertainty; information and commu-
nication are perhaps the only strategic weapons now available to humanity for combating exploitation, ignorance and oppression...*

(contemporary black thought)

Intelligence has always been on the forefront in predicting and
determining the dynamism of every leadership, thus, it is addicted
to understanding, communication, and the application of information. Intelligence is a required tool to articulate change and adapt
to it. However, its acumen is simply acquired by learning from how
passed events were presented, because every desired outcome of
every event has a deliberate preparation and processed input.
Hence, how we prepare is important; who we trust to be in the
fore front, to lead and guide is also very important. Leadership
and intelligence are two different concepts that needs to be tackled together in order to highlight their very essence. Leadership
transforms and intelligence revolves; the combination of both is

strategic to serve obliquely in contending the unknown or what is coming...The future!

Our world is evolving continuously, which requires that the core decisions should be made by those who have proper understanding and sufficient bearing for the coming era. The world is becoming more eccentric with the continuous emerging advancement of technology, smart tools, artificial intelligence, robotics, machine learning, computation, IoT and so on. Therefore leadership intelligence must be in step with adaptability and innovation.

Adaptability is an intuitive resolution; and for any person, group, society and organization to keep up with pace and keep surviving, that entity must continually keep track of the flow of emerging innovations. Change will always be traced back to the thinkers of every generation, those that lived in their minds, such as innovators, trailblazers, and pathfinders in their various fields. These people's abilities, visions, ideas, transform and inspire others even to the generations after them.   Leadership intelligence can be evaluated in terms of certain determinant quotients, and I will discuss some below.

Intelligent quotient;   IQ is an academic tool use in assessing a person's mental capabilities. This assesses basically language and logic using cognitive abilities such as memory, attention and speed. Intelligence quotient, IQ profiling is the distinction of individuals made through academic assessment, and it has garnered popularity. It is measured and expressed in numbers, and when it is low, a person is referred to as having low IQ. An individual's IQ number can be obtained through a test with a set average determined from the marks of previous test takers. When you undergo this test relatively to your age and your answer is above the set average, then you are considered smart but if your number is lower than the set average, you are not considered smart after all.

It is the ratio of mental age (Ma) as a ratio of the chronological age (Ca) multiplied by 100 (i.e. IQ = Ma/Ca). Irrespective of dulling IQ effect, it is believe that there are some factors that is related to why some children falls short; prenatal exposure to alcohol, cognitive impairment due to early exposure to ill health during child's developmental stage, trauma and so on. But IQ as important as it may sound doesn't determine the future mandate of an individual, because academic profiling can only inhibit one based on academic quest but all other life endeavours may not need an academic mind. In fact, leadership only needs one's willingness to lead.

'*Small Me*' is clever and he doesn't want anybody seeking him out from his 'hide and seek' game. He believes that there is no need of talking or learning about IQ when it's not for him; it brings up this feeling of resentment, IQ was one of the enemies that made him erect a wall a long time ago. He hates to lose and fail, why then should he learn about a tool that will flash it on his face every time? ... "I am not impaired in my mental capabilities but as long as it's for measuring academic performances, that is not a tool I want to learn about".

To provide a balance, why does high IQ matter, if it's a tool for discrimination between people of different learning abilities? There are so many other life endeavours that can be affected positively and achieved without academic excellence. Therefore, it is important to know that empathy and emotional intelligence is a preferable profiling tool.

Emotional intelligence; This is a constant check and control of our emotion. Our temperament is the determinant scale. Losing our temper shows low EQ; but even when we experience anger but manage to control our reaction demonstrates a high EQ.

I learnt a great lesson on EQ during one of our match days in my early days in football coaching career. My team was in this game playing so well and we were winning at that moment but I was still on the edge; the game was not yet over. At one moment, the opposing team was attacking on our half of the field, but I had my striking player tactically waiting close to the mid-line for a rebound, in case of a quick counter attack to get us more goals. The next thing I saw was that he was being deliberately punched on his face but the referee didn't see it because he was focused on the area of action. I manage to get his attention to pause the game, before I ran to help my boy on the ground who was struggling with pain. But then I did what I was not supposed to do, I'd caution the boy who punched my player in the face never to do that again instead of going over to talk to his coach and express my concern. I had completely forgotten it was a minor's game due to excess unease and passion. The boy who punched my player started crying, maybe out of his own guilt feeling or because of the manner by which I cautioned him. Immediately, I realized that I might have gone way out of line. Of course, I became 'a bad coach', my job is to build them up not to break them down. At the end, winning the game didn't matter anymore and I had to openly apologize to the parents that were present and to every other person around for my inappropriate action, especially to the young boy and I encouraged him to see my action as another plea to keep playing fair.

I demonstrated a low EQ; it doesn't matter the person involved, be it a minor or an adult. To be a leader (coach, teacher), it is your responsibility to lead by example. I have since been constantly fine tuning my emotional intelligence skills as it is important if I am to succeed in the field and society at large. It is every leaders' and everyone's responsibility to demonstrate a high EQ, because our society and organization needs it in order to continue finding lasting solutions to every upcoming challenges. There should be a pattern of observation, patience, and introspection, which will bring harmony to self (MEs') in such a way there will be no guilty conscience or regrets after any action. EQ maybe very impossible without empathy. We are social beings as our lives involve other people. Empathy is demonstrated when you are able to share in other people's feelings.

"Empathy is maturity" said Daniel Goleman, "it's a virtue." Leaders, coaches, and everyone need to have empathy. It's a show of high EQ. If you evaluate your emotions via your actions, and you are sure you are not high in EQ, I think it is important that you begin to learn it. Emotional intelligence is a learnable skill. Maybe you are the missing piece of the solution as the world is virtually becoming smaller and our cultures are merging intelligently.

Cultural intelligence; As the world is becoming smaller as a result of tourism, immigration and technology (internet), we meet people from almost everywhere in the world on a daily basis both online and in person. Every person we meet has a behavior/attitude moulded by their culture and this portrays their values. Technology having brought our world so close, and we having to adapt in such a 'small' space, it is important that we know how to overcome our biases. This will ensure that everyone is in the same frame of mind as we all work together towards building up our society and world in general.

Culture is the people's way of life. Families do have their own culture, so does the society. Learning other people's culture enables one to be able to fit in that society and knowing the way to operate. For healthy relationships to occur between any two or more people, they must endeavour to understand each other's culture in order to be able to undermine biases and differences that may generate disagreements. Sorting through cultural differences might be a daunting task but quitting is not what you should opt for; well, cultural intelligence demands that we go beyond our comfort boundaries to learn and adjust.

According to Julia Middleton, cultural intelligence is the ability to cross boundaries and borders between different cultures and thrive. She explained that, the edge cultural intelligence has over emotional intelligence is that you also have to deal with people that are not just like you. Cultural intelligence is the lens through which we perceive the world. It's important to help us unified our world and overcome biases. First, it's about you developing your own personal culture; establishing what is important to you and what is less important to you. Of course it's your drive, knowledge, action, and strategy.

Our society is indeed a bowel mixed with different people and class, your ability to navigate well depends on your internal or external feeling about the next person around you. Are you passionate about meeting new people or doing something in order to impress other people?

How you mix up with people shows how adaptable you are about their culture depending on how similar or dissimilar their culture is to yours. To maintain relationships with people, your values are important both to you and to them. Your action will reveal how much you respect other people's values. And if you do not undertake it carefully, of course your cultural intelligence is low, but if you take it up with carefulness, it shows that your cultural intelligence is high. One needs a plan and awareness to deal with other people; it's strategic because you never know all their intents. Cultural Intelligence involves assessment of trust that assures me that my values are safe and respected before revealing to anyone; no one wants to be ridiculed. People like to follow a leader who is leading them differently; someone who understands different cultures with no bias and prejudice.

Business intelligence; Every day, people go about their businesses, traveling, schooling, shopping, sleeping, partying, and driving around the city. Life involves people engaging in different transactions, and the outcome depends on their decision making. Business intelligence is all about decision making. Business is simply an exchange of goods and service between two or more parties. It attracts the values of the commodity in exchange.

Back in the day, trade was done by a system called barter; an example would be a piece or shekel of gold for a shekel of silver or two shekels of silver depending on the value attached to those items or a drum of oil to a full roll of cotton fabrics. But in the wakes, as time passes due to necessity, money in form of gold coin or any other piece of fine metal was introduced. Money was an enabler for trade to be fair among all the parties. When one doesn't have the item another wants, it will be easier for them to pay in coin, and the one having the coin can go over and acquire what they actually want. Today, technology has advanced money, mode of transactions, and payments in today's market via digital transfers, although cash money is still in circulation. Some now even invest in cryptocurrency. Business keeps evolving as style of payment keeps advancing but trading remains at the root of it all.

Business structures are continually changing due to competition and desires. Competition is the force that enables and pushes innovation forward while desire drives demand. Many businesses are in different circumstances today depending on the kind of leadership they have been entrusted to lead. We have learned that as time changes, innovation advances, but goals, missions and culture of every organization remains the pivot. Smart business leaders are quick to make sound decisions in other to keep their businesses sustainable. Technology, artificial intelligence, robotics are all here and they all have overwhelming effects in every area. What decisions are leaders making in other to ensure sustainability of their businesses? Are those decisions sound enough to create and sustain sound profit margins for the company's growth? Business advancement is a non-stop moving train due to innovation. You can either try to keep up with the right decision making, and adapt to the changes or you will be left behind. In every growing and sustainable business, leaders with the right decision making skills form a key factor. Their business intelligence comes into play as they navigate the changes happening around; both in internal and external facets of the organization.

Artificial intelligence; This is the key driver of automation. Automation itself has been in existence long before now. Humans have always had tools to help in easing their work; from simple tools like hoes, shovel, and screw driver to big automatic machines. But the need for perfection still pushes for more through research in science and technology.

Brigette Hyacinth, in her book "The future of leadership"- (Rise of automation, robotics and artificial intelligence) diligently detailed what she perceives as the future; she agrees that artificial intelligence is pushing boundaries of our human imagination. She also went on to explain that artificial intelligence, AI and robots are not the same but they are often merged together in achieving a common goal. Robots are hardwares and AI is software, in the real sense. Artificial Intelligence is a written algorithm that can mimic some human functions. When a machine exhibits human intelligence like having simple interactions, dancing, serving in a restaurant and performing some checks, in some cases their performance are faster, better, and time efficient. Artificial intelligence and robots will of course never replace humans. We have instincts which drives our inconsistency, adaptability, and behavioral patterns; meaning that we are lots less predictable whereas robots are predictable and well known for their particular functions.

Artificial intelligence is growing steadily; innovation is matching up and exceeding human capability in some areas. Artificial intelligence has posed questions due to growing number of people losing their jobs, time after time, as companies relieve people of their jobs as they increasingly automate their operations. How much damage will artificial intelligence continue to cause, due to it cost effectiveness? Leadership of the future should be concerned with providing lasting solutions for dire persisting and daring human problems, including the danger of artificial intelligence. Most challenges we face are those of the mind due to fear, indeed, every challenge thrown at us is actually aimed at our minds. The aim is to cause people to sway their minds, and to inject fear; the more they fear, the more they lose hope and confidence in their own self. We are always fighting to protect our mind; the mind is a battle field.

Leaders should be able to find a balance between human function and machine function, because if we allow machines to invade every aspect of our daily lives, it then means that our existence maybe in for ruin. Although automation and artificial intelligence maybe proving cost effective, yield less emotional stress, and more on point, yet human efficacy is still a thing of value. So leadership intelligence is applicable to every area of human existence. It must be indulged in at all times to ensure maximum benefit to mankind.

Leadership intelligence based on religion; Religion is a practice anchored on beliefs. We are all believers in something or in some-one. The difference is in who or what, and how we practice our belief in form of devotion and supplication. It is an affair believed to have a connection between the physical and spiritual, and it has played a vital role in human history and humanity. Man has always sought for his life purpose, meaning, and the very essence of liv-ing. In response, religion has always pointed towards the invisible; an existing higher being that controls our affairs. Religion also has played vital role in leadership observations and obligations.

Religion and leadership are inseparable affairs of men; men have always believed in the certainty of a higher order. Every religion believes that there is a God and by faith, we have a moral obliga-tion to do the right things in other for us to meet the invisible af-ter life (this is the consolation of all our morals).

Knowing the right thing to do is for the benefit of every one and doing the good thing is usually for personal reasons. This as stated earlier is the distinction between my '*Big Me*' doing what is right and '*Small Me*' doing what is good. Spiritual intelligence is serving higher purpose other than self, and patriotism is serving unbiased and relentlessly towards the course of other people and the nation. Spiritual intelligence helps in managing different religious practices. It's important that we highlight its importance as our society is strongly influenced by our collective belief system. For us to be able to co-exist, we must know how to respect each other and how not to infringe on people's right with respect to their belief. Leaders who are spiritually intelligent usually oversee the affair of their followers with high level of dignity, transparency, accountability and honesty thereby creating a room for tolerance, and undermining bias. It's important to understand religion and have spiritual intelligence in order for us to ease the tension that may arise due to differences in belief. The world has an enormous number of people with a spirituality and adhering to one religious believe or another. Even within a religion, there are sects who agree on some beliefs and disagree on some; sentiments exists giving rise to bigotry and fanaticism. Bigotry and fanaticism doesn't show intelligence nor tolerance, and unfortunately they have tendencies of creating and escalating violence, hate, fighting, and division among adherents.

Religious leaders with understanding of volatility and fragility of religious sentiments usually promote messages of peace, unity and love. Such messages are in effect to break barriers of a particular doctrine and dogma. Leaders in the religious sector should also be able to adopt intelligence not only to cross boundaries and to quench tension, but develop avenues for adaptation in order to keep in step with changing times as some religious practice may become archaic, obsolete, and untenable.

7

LEADERSHIP PATTERN

Matters of the heart is in abundance, and overwhelming
…love is an attraction from the last chamber…
It is the core,
And in abundance
The paradigm of light aligns in colors

Sands' in grain
Ripples over the water
Wings above skies…
For love is a draw to purpose
We soar, because we soar
They crawl for they crawl
Having everything in order,

For love is a draw for purpose
It clears doubt
Yet, things are meant to be
However, you chose it to happen
Intentionally or not
The sky remains high
And we tread upon gravel
But our peace is our peace
And should be our peace.

(In the shadow of my mind,2020) Chinedu Darlington

"…I'm rather out of my depth in such affairs but I'll say this, there are neither proofs nor underlying laws that can determine the outcomes of the matters of the heart, of this I'm sure…" Hardy expressing thoughtfully his heart to his dear friend Ramanudjan, in the motion picture 2015 film "(The man who knew infinite)."

As in every other significant order of things, leadership depicts patterns in growth and transformation. It's a progressive reeling that aligns with natural laws for transformation, and it is all aimed at bringing about change. Change happens all the time with a pattern, so also leadership has a pattern. Leadership pattern is a model for mental growth, which can reproduce as a result of our attitude. Change can occur in different directions, and which direction it goes has a lot to do with how we perceive things. The outcome of change also depends on the input; an input of empathy and love would yield admiration and positive mental growth, whereas an approach with apathy most definitely will yield otherwise. Positive mental growth starts from one being able to commit to one's self and staying committed. If you remain committed, resilient and never to fail yourself in your own endeavor, you will surely win while others can then benefit from and emulate you.

But that doesn't come so easily without discipline, which is the best organic manure for mental growth. I do not believe that discipline can be instilled by punishment, subjection, deprivation or denial rather it demands one to be intentional in all necessary actions. Discipline is a skill; a learnable skill. Of course, it's not everybody's nature to be disciplined. Discipline is an outcome of learning, training and practicing to the extent that your actions becomes devoid of mediocrity and bias. It requires that one should always consider all sides of a situation before making a conscious decision. Decisions of our heart are the drive of every leadership pattern and should be directed towards humanity and liberation.

Anyways, humanity is also about liberty, and in its very essence appreciates leadership pattern as an agent of change. So, it is a call for change, as change remains inevitable over time. Leadership pattern has moved from the tough tightened fist of an absolute monarch to the general hands of the people. Where everyone is represented, meaning that leadership has evolved from dominance to inclusion. Dominance is a proud show of superiority, and it favors other elements such as coercion, exclusion, and control. It still exists in our world today due to insensitivity and lack of mind evolution among some people in authority. Such classes of people have always through their wealth and level of education showcased themselves among us in form of elitism and classism. Thereby having those assumed uninformed or lesser beings relegated from their circle of interaction.

Inclusive leadership has changed the whole dynamics of leadership patterns. The inclusive leadership model achieves faster growth by bringing together and making everyone responsible. Inclusive leadership allows for views that everyone may not agree to; it allows for disagreement on issues, yet, it requires that every decision taken should still positively impact at least the majority. It values differences and commonality in everybody regardless of their background, gender, sexual orientation, race, tribe, and so on. Inclusion values both uniqueness and belongingness. Uniqueness is what distinguishes an individual from a crowd, and belongingness is the feeling of acceptance within a group, as related in course lecture on "21st century leaders, facilitated by catalyst.org, 2017."

Inclusive leadership is the present era for leadership as it thrives on collaboration and delegation. These are the very key for any group or organization to achieve their vision and success. Some organizations are made up of people with differences in concepts and perception due to their colour, gender, sexual orientation, race, abilities, and creed, but the common ground of no discrimination brings everyone together by their own merit. I believe that it's an open invitation for everyone to come and achieve their purpose. Inclusion is a leadership pattern birthed out of necessity due to diversity, but the common goal is provision of solutions. Being able to provide solutions is the broker for one to become relevant.

The dynamism for achieving a pattern of leadership is something that has been present all through human existence. Men survived the odd in caves, and ran naked on cold arctic mountains and in the wild. Survival instinct has always been a prevalent tool for adaptation then and even now; same for other animals and living creatures. To remain adaptable, our instincts should be alive and alert at all times, ensuring our intuition remains proactive. Being proactive should be motivated by precaution and not induced by fear. Precautionary motives must be based on research and must be in line with past experiences. For example, if we anticipate summer, then we'll prepare for summer. Also, we lock our doors as a precaution against intruders.

Events may be minor or major depending on the conventional source and perception. Summer might result in higher temperatures than anticipated, or even after locking your doors, burglars can gain access through the air duct. This might sound minor because it is common. But let's say there is an outbreak of war, plague in a city or even in the entire world just like the Coronavirus (COVID 19), any of these major events will most definitely change the way we live swiftly as it will shift the dynamism of leadership. Our expectations will change as our priorities are re-ordered. For example, His Highness Sheik Mohammed the ruler of Dubai related that the outbreak of corona virus has exposed that nothing else matters more than our health care system.

A simple analogy of leadership pattern is cause and effect. It is a prescription that helps all leaders with faster decision making and direction. Events occur and leave behind an aftermath for us to deal with a new sense of realization. World War II left the world devastated and humanity responded with formation of United Nations in 1945 in order to tackle issues of global peace, and its sustainability. This was to ensure that an issue like war can be dealt with in a mutual and peaceful way. As safety is everyone's priority, it's only natural for us to always adopt basic precautionary measures, some of which are listed below;

X. *Forming a group or alliance:* this has so many benefits, at least we feel safer in a pack, rather than being a lone ranger. When a group is formed, their main aim is to stay together and face every challenge together. Our safety is always a priority for us as humans.

X. *Establishing a safe zone:* Sometimes, our first instinct in the face of danger is simply to flee, a preventive measure proving the quote "live to fight another day". For instance, the stay home and stay safe measure during the Corona virus pandemic

X. *Creating a defensive tool:* Challenges can come in the form of an attack. Our natural response will be to defend, which may be to use improvised tools are as a support to our strength, so that we can face the challenge squarely.

It is also important to note that major positive events which include innovations have also shifted the dynamics of our world in various areas. Innovations in various areas have brought about revolutions at different times, and only adaptable leadership can react fast enough so as to enjoy the value added by these innovations. Invention of aircraft by Wright brothers, computers, telephones, internet, and even machineries came from the place of hard labor. And only fast adapting people and organizations are able to enjoy its early dividends of ease at performance, doing work and cost efficiency. Of course with time, the dividend trickles down to everyone and shifts the dynamics of things. Leadership pattern has no single formula, it's just a dynamic force of one's perception and attitude towards every given event and opportunity in society.

In conclusion, it may not be very clear if dynamism of the present day virtual engagement has completely done away with physical offices and physical engagement in organizations, but gradually, working remotely or virtually is rapidly gaining grounds. I can only say that the creativity side of this leadership pattern is intentionally disrupting the tradition and culture of organizational leadership patterns.

8

LEADERSHIP PRINCIPLE OF SUCCESS

"Success is deliberate…"

What is success? Depending on one's perspective, success could have one of many definitions. Success is a process that aligns one to achieve a set goal or goals. Achieving a goal does not necessarily make you successful rather; it sets you up for a higher challenge. Being successful is not a showcase of accomplishment; instead it's a relentless effort at accomplishing more, providing more value in order to serve humanity better and generously. Serving humanity is about communicating value to others, and that is what portrays your leadership brand. Yes, leadership is not a label but the way you influence others gives a brand to your service, for example political leader, captain, coach, teacher, and so on.

Branding or your brand as a leader may determine or catalyze how successful you will become while you are serving, because it will project you relative to the value you are adding. Added value is subjective to perception. For instance, the way people perceive your services can create a shift in their mindset. It is called influencing. However, not everybody will really appreciate you, because they may not have conceived any beneficial value in their minds that can be attributed to your service. That does not mean there is any problem with your service or approach. However, success in any endeavor is deliberate and a continuously gradual process. Therefore, the first and the only principle of success is to become a leader, and the last principle is to remain a leader. Every successful person knows that assuming their roles as leaders gives them leverage of becoming a success, but that is not without an obvious cost. Leadership is gifted with life lessons and experiences that are useful, and if understood, will give you a deeper insight on the best way of becoming successful.

Leadership starts with taking charge of your life. This may sound delusional but like an adage once said, "you can take a horse to the stream but you can't force the horse to drink." I said that because everything lies first in your decision, meaning that no one can make you succeed if you aren't willing to succeed. Your success awaits you only when you are ready to embrace it. Leading yourself may mean digging up some of your buried potentials, experiences, and start putting them to use. It may mean to actively secure a gainful employment. I'm not the kind of motivator that will tell you not to work at a job for somebody because it is derogatory, what matters most is the value you are putting in and receiving either in form of learning, relearning a skill, developing a passion that will eventually be profitable, learning adaptation, and how to navigate through challenges.

For me as a person, I'd deflated myself by allowing situations to shut me down until I realized that no one was going to come to my rescue. I then decided that I will re-invent myself, face the challenges ahead, and humble myself by dealing with my ego as it hadn't done me any good. I decided to use a gift I knew that was in me... the knowledge of the game I have played all my life. Of course, I had to start learning more and developing me to become a football coach. Although the path was never an easy route to follow, it has definitely been a journey worth daring. Today, I'm a licensed football/soccer coach and the journey is still ongoing. I remember trying to talk myself out of my personal journey to development, but the urge to succeed surpassed the pain and shame of quitting, and the feeling of worthlessness that would eventually arise. Today, I do have a better feeling in life and in myself because I am of the service to people and that's what leaders do! In fact, that's what successful people do! Leaders service with vision.

Taking leadership of your life or endeavors is not something quite easy to do; external forces against you are as magnified as internal voices speaking all along the way. Rejection can be a good gift in your journey to success. It may be the most common thing you will encounter on your road to success, but never let it turn you down or off, rather use it as a catalyst to push forward. I'd started off with no experience in football coaching and I did not play the game professionally. Guess what I did? I offered to work with a dear friend of mine on the job for free as long as I can learn to become a coach. It was a positive mental shift for me. During those periods, whenever I wanted to quit due to adversity or discouragement, I would simply remind myself of the reason why I started the journey in the first place. One time, I remember encouraging myself that one of the greatest coaches like Jose Mourinho did not requisitely played as a professional footballer.

As success is a product of continuous learning and development from your experience, you must have to be rational and radical in making your choices. To re-invent requires you to embrace and understand what I call the R3 factor; Revelation, Rebellion and Revolution. The R3-factor is a tool that can present limitless possibilities and opportunities.

Revelation; nothing reveals to us the need for change more than pain. Nobody likes to deal with pain but it's an indicator to us that there is a need for change. Just the thought of a past painful experience can make a wise person more proactive. It makes him to pause and think about the present situation or a forth coming one. This is referred to as realization or cognitive revelation. It is a calculated and clear understanding of one's situation, knowing the reality, the challenges and the possible solution. When your pain becomes evident, that is the conception and awareness period, knowing the cause and the effect will be a clear motivation to prevent its reoccurrence.

Rebellion; This can be referred to, as one's refusal to accept a threatening dire situation. At some point, we need to rebel against our old habit of talking our self out of our dreams or out of the process towards our liberty. Our reasons for an action should be stronger than the contrary voices. When I started off as coach, I usually get out of bed by 5.00am every weekend to change into my coaching uniform and set out to work. It was seriously against my comfort and bordered on rebellion. I remember vividly that on those days I wasn't on the pay list, but it was the sacrifice needed for me to learn discipline that I would need as a coach. Football knowledge alone was not enough; coaching is much more than having players running around under your instruction with a ball on the pitch. It's a leadership position, and if I must excel in it, I must do the needful. And besides, it was obvious everybody was watching...

Revolution; this is usually found in the place of knowing exactly what you are aiming for, your course of action, and been committed to carrying them out. It entails discipline and perseverance no matter the difficulties faced. During the time my job got terminated a day after the incident, I cautioned a boy for hitting one of my boys on the face inside the pitch, I got discouraged about coaching. I thought of quitting and giving up everything. In fact, sometimes, the easiest thing someone can do is to quit. However, after a long thought, I realized that I had come a long way to just allow a single mistake to put me down and out.

I had to fight an inner battle to shut out that inner voice telling me to quit. The world out there may say bad things, but the inner voice could be saying worse things. Of course, not being emotional intelligent enough in that moment was entirely my fault and the best thing to do was to fix it. I was not an impostor on the sidelines; I learned my craft and was qualified even though I am still learning more on a daily basis. It took me months even as a professional to get an unpaid assistant coaching position elsewhere; but as long as I was learning, I didn't mind. I proceeded to undertake a further professional training under the UAE Football Association, which granted me an Asian football confederation license that entitles me as a fully licensed coach. You see, I revolted by owning my mistake, downplayed my ego and shame, even apologized openly for my mistake, and waited for that period to phase out... as it is said, time heals all wounds. Ever since then, I have being empathic on my feet everyday doing what I love, coaching except for this period of total lockdown due to Coronavirus pandemic, which interestingly has given me the opportunity to pen this book down. R3 factor is all about breaking the bond of odds against our success by taking responsibility.

9

RECEIVING

"When you refuse to receive, you are arrogant."

Comedian Michael jr.

… What do you have that you did not receive? …

1 Corinthian 4: 7

Receiving is a great phenomenon that supports the principle of success. Receiving doesn't come before giving, neither does giving come after receiving. They are both concurrent actions in an infinite cycle. Receiving is usually viewed but wrongly so as inferior while giving is seen as a thing of pride, and superior to receiving. However, receiving is as important as giving.

Receiving is an acceptance of trust that whatever it is will be passed on in same form or in another form to someone else. Certain concepts must co-exist, for instance, positive charge can never be positive charge if there is no negative charge to compliment it. So does most of other concepts like, tall and short, right and wrong, better and worse, big and small, the list can go on and on.

But we always laud the one that feels good and derogates the other, and it is simply subjective-based biases.

There will be no receiving if there is no giving, they happen concurrently and there should be no prejudice. It is one of life's ultimate principles. We are always in need and always desiring for something but most times, we are not ready to receive. My gut to start from the reverse (receiving) is how and where I'd learnt leadership from being an observing and active follower. My intention is not to create bias, but to clear the notion that only the assumed credible can receive the mandate to lead.

Receiving means adding to one's collections. It can have both transformational and transactional implications. Every exchange is as a result of a relationship, and they are built on trust. Relationships flourish on the grounds of mutual understanding and benefit... giving and receiving or offering and taking. Healthy relationships thrive on how well we understand this concept of giving and receiving; it's as simple as the first law of motion "action and reaction are equal and opposite". In business, every party comes to the table to negotiate for their own interest and when every party gets what they want, it is a win-win for all. This concept also applies to romantic relationship; when you give absolute love, you receive absolute love.

In contrary, discord in a relationship among couples or in other aspects of our lives are actually in tune with 'offering and taking'; transactional without empathy. This is akin to negotiating only for spaces rather than understanding our places. It obviously shows when we do not understand the whole principle of receiving and giving. Such misunderstandings leads to disagreement and breakups; people end up maybe without a win in form of a win-lose or lose-lose situation. Businesses and indeed everyone needs relationships in order to thrive. From my understanding, most lonely people do not know how to receive people into their lives; maybe I'm wrong but I speak from my experience. I know some people will want to disagree with me, but you might be a receiver and your partner is a taker or you may be a giver and your partner is an offerer. Interpersonal skills and excellent "customer" service are crucial in any relationship as it shows a receptive disposition.

Healthy relationships can boost our psychology and change our behavioral pattern from being failure-prone to being success-prone. It has the tendency to help us handle negative attitudes towards ourselves. Often times, we are the ones self-sabotaging our own efforts by playing low when we're supposed to play high. This maybe as a result of fear of failure or for whatever other reasons you deems fit. It could be conscious or unconscious bringing imbalance rather than harmonization. Healthy relationships are therefore important for genuine success. Some habits that can make way for self-sabotage are discussed below;

Unhealthy habits; everyone wants to be in company of someone with good character. However, sound character is formed from a long chain of sound concepts starting with habits and then behavior. For instance, nobody wants to go out on a date with a person with bad eating habit to prevent any embarrassing events that may occur while out.

Personal bias; at one time or another we have judged people even before we met them based on a bias we have. It's an internal representation of who we are, and that always show in our attitude, which could be self-sabotaging.

Unforgiveness; forgive yourself, this is something we all need to do for ourselves as we are all dealing with issues from our past, which could keep getting the better part of us. Forgiving others is another huge mile stone, because unforgiveness is an immature thing to do against one's self and others. It lowers the level of your harmony. And when one is in a poor state of harmony, their level of energy is low. That means your attitude towards your productivity could be affected in a negative way. This could also affect our interpersonal relationship with others.

Distraction; this is a very dangerous habit when allowed to run rouge especially in children. As a habit, it permeates into a lot of areas manifesting in form of excess playing, and lack of attention, which will affect their ability to learn and comprehend. It leads to formation of poor learning stamina, which is pure self-sabotage. Adults infuse distraction with things like alcoholism or some sort, which may lead to abuse if not controlled. In an adult it is called self-distract, which may be a mechanism to turn away pain for a moment. Self-distraction is a common tool we all engage, and how we use them is a determinant on how we progress. Distraction can be beneficial if one can find how to use it properly or learn to embrace it in a creative way.

Display of ignorance; whether your action is on purpose or not, people's attitude towards you is always in response to the action you put forth for them to see. Ignorance is not an excuse, and unguarded or uninformed utterances will usually attract shame. Therefore all our utterances and actions should be informed by facts and well-articulated before execution. Everyone wants to associate with people of the same level of articulation and learn from people with more careful and thoughtful self-presentation...

there are many other factors that can put people away from you but may not be relevant to our subject matter at the moment.

Offer is important for negotiations (Advantage); Offer and take may seem unhealthy in this context, but it's important to note that there are tough grounds of negotiations where the transactional approach may be the only plausible choice left through which an agreement can be reached. Negotiation is apparently a form of exchange; if it is handled well, it will always end in every body's favor, or it sure will end in a win-loss or even a loss-loss. Negotiating power stems from self-worth and self-believe… if you think you don't have negotiation power, it means you either do not know your full worth or you are lacking in self-believe. Negotiation can also be valuable in conflict resolution as an alternative to confrontation; although confrontation does not necessarily have to be aggressive and negative. Avoiding confrontation is not how to keep peace. Conflicts are only a natural part of our relationships, personal growth, and life journey.

KNOW YOUR SEED

…While the earth remains, seed time and harvest shall not cease…

(Genesis 8:22)

Success is not a myth; I believe it aligns with the universal law of sowing and leaping. It has processes and strategies. Your seed is not the whole but a fraction of your earnings. My father loved farming; yearly, he cultivated tubers and crops of different kinds. After harvest, he stores up the crops and tubers in a local made storage facility called barn, which has a section where a fraction of the harvest is kept as seedlings for the next farming season. According to him, it's important to know the size of your seed, it is equally important to know when and where to sow.

In our world today, most people don't undertake small scale farming but in a practical term, our jobs and businesses are our farms. Our salary and the profit we make at the end of a period is like my dad's harvest. If one receives his pay check, it's important that your first thought should be what percentage will be my savings (seed). I don't mean savings for delayed expenses but for reinvestment. Financial management should be a compulsory preoccupation for everyone. Financial lessons are well thought by many but 'Big dad, Small dad' by Robert Kiyosaki was the eye opener for me. I admire his work so much because he advises that you should be able to save up at least 10 percent of you income as a seed for investment.

AVOID YOUR DISTRACTION

"…the mark of a person who is in control of consciousness is the ability to focus attention at will, to be oblivious to distractions, to concentrate for as long as it will take to achieve a goal, and no longer…"

Mihaly Csikszentmilalyi

I grew up using distraction as a tool to avoid pain, although not entirely endorsed by my 'B*ig Me*' now, it was necessary at the time for my survival. People normally consider distraction as been negative and want nothing to do with it, but believe me, a good number of us are addicted to it in the same way as nicotine, caffeine, and other life harmful agents.

A society with high levels of distraction resulting in unintentionality, inadequate learning and understanding especially among the children will end up with a high number of low creativity individuals. When the level of creativity is low, it will definitely affect the quality of leadership, the economy, and many other things. Creating a suitable learning environment for children is therefore important.

Distraction is not all negative; it can be put to a positive use. It could be a rebounding mechanism but must be employed appropriately. The difference between an A-level kid and the loser kid is how they learn to use distraction. Distraction is an emotional and unseen tool. Kids that give to high levels of distraction find it difficult to learn, whereas kids with appropriate levels of distraction find it easy to learn. Distraction can also be an issue in adults; people push forward things that are meant to be done not because they are busy, but because they lack the audacity to tackle them at that moment. This is distraction playing out in form of procrastination. Maintaining focus requires willpower and it's a skill everyone needs to learn. Listening and focusing is a valuable attribute; it grants one the ability to take in more information and retain it for future use. Focus must be on things that matters and not on irrelevant things.

10

LEADERSHIP POETRY

...Leadership is about been authentic and real...

Bill Clinton.
(Former President of the United States of America.)

A MOTHER'S LAMENT

With sorrow she approached me, to speak of her son.
She seemed a broken soul, mistreated by him

She thought that he valued her so dearly,
he who was part of her flesh and being.

Wounded, she came to me when her hopes had been dashed,
she came with pain that no time could measure.

She said: "After his father's abrupt demise,
I took care of him, and raised him so dearly...

An orphan with no place for shelter,
A mere infant, sleeping in his cradle...

For his sake, I took up a servant's job,
Hoping night's promise would someday be fulfilled…

Years went by, and he grew into a man,
The day I awaited had finally arrived."

She paused right then, with silent tears,
Running down her cheeks, her pain I could see

With a broken voice, she spoke once again,
Of how he threw her out of the place they called home.

At first I kept silent, my soul was enraged,
By the cruelty and injustice, brought upon her.

I said to her: "Your right was denied *as if in a lion's den,*
They will be returned to you, after the beast's defeat…"

With an intention to help in such difficult times,
I called for him, to reprimand his wrong-doing.

My words were interrupted by her pleading voice:
"What are you doing?" She asked with a startled tone.

I am his Mother, sir, do not condemn him.
How can a mother's heart oppress her own child?"

How vast is her forgiveness, how tender is her heart?
When empowered she pardoned and forgot his cruel deeds.

H.H. Sheik. Mohammed Bin Rashid Al Maktoum
(Poems from the Desert)

His Highness narrated motherhood at her very best. He painted her nature of kind-heartedness and divine purpose as she accentuated purpose to humanity with a demonstration of an unconditional love for her children. Leaders that will ever flourish must learn their paradigm and purpose from "her" over time.

Leadership is about humanity.

This piece lured my tenderness
As hardened and complex as I am
Made by nature
Yet, I have learned to pardon and forget
The cruelty of all offenses…

The voice is strong and words are powerful
Like a garden, so is our heart,
Whatever we hear is a seed or a weed,
That which we learn is righteous to plant.
Then our tongue speaks life,
Our poetry is that righteous plant of our heart
Sieved from among em' weeds

Poetry exposes our vulnerability, and the authentic part of our tender and chaotic minds. According to President Clinton's call to be authentic, a leader is also a human with wit to stand in for. In the stanza below; leaders bleeds.

The reality is that leaders feel what others feel or even more. We all have fears in the face of uncertainty, and tranquility in the face of certainty. The world we build was first built in our minds; before the blue print was a blood print of subconscious reality. Leaders who envisioned their world in detail expresses it in a contextual form that represents its worthiness. We worry but necessity gives birth to creativity.

Leaders bleed blood
Their ordinance is of no ease
They stay awake to tame our gardens,
Weed our beds of many flowers,
Watch the night sky in serenity.
They wonder, in awe of the night sky.
The moon,
Stars of flame,
And yet they wonder.

Our universe is a field, expanse in detailed partitions of amazing terrain of dimensional elements, which are interdependent over each other, like the air, the water, the fire and the earth.

The principle that guides us as human maybe spiritual or holistic or maybe divine, but the essence of living is to find peace and happiness. Yet, they are the rarest and scarcely.

Then what are we searching for?
Most can not see but they have eyes,
many can not stand but they have legs,
many can not lift their fingers if not to point towards a blame.
Knowing peace of mind, is in the finding the relevance we long.
It is that finding voice we lost,
the potency is in our abilities,
then shall our joy spring.

Our world has known no peace and tranquillity for the fear of the unknown. Change confronts fear, yet many would not learn how to adapt. A poetry sets a bunch of words free from the tender heart of a leader. For they speak of wisdom. Leaders who speaks words of wisdom, does so on the dais of higher order. It is not a height so easy to attain but in brilliance. Men of higher order shape the world as we know it, but first they sharp their minds. Their voice is heard from the manifestation of their courage and handmade. Leader's prophetic pronouncement is poetic, and from a measured and strategic vision.

Narratives say a story and send a message along in verses, even in choruses. Fear picks both the brave and the cowards alike, but the brave stand in its face courageously, as the cowards run into hiding.

Vision may come first but of what purpose will it serve for my people? This is a sincere thought of responsibility and obligation that transcend from a troubled heart of a leader.

If the purpose of a vision is to divide, not finding the right balance, be it equality, equity, it is not deserved. Humanity stands for all human races. Inclusion is the grease, building bridges not walls, breaking barrier, standing against differences, inequality, biases, stereotype, oppression, racism and so on.

After listening to my heart questions…

'*Small Me*': In that case, why has the world been so cruel…especially to children?

'B*ig Me*': His Highness's narrative is a painting of preservation… though her heart bleeds, she did not come to condemn rather even when empowered, she pardoned and forgave

'*Small Me*'; Just that?

'Big Me': hope in the vision, it sees beyond our horizon. It is to bring a better world of peace and harmony...and if that is defeated...then the vision maybe tyrannical. And don't forget that even those men ahead are vulnerable and human too.

'Small Me': What?!

'BigMe': Another thing, mothers/women could be more attune in raising a more transformational leaders than men do, though men have more guts to create empires and their managers.

CONCLUSION

When you scale your whole life on a pivot of conscience then will you realize how much you have wasted or gained on the area of decision making. Decision making is a compass of navigation for leadership's sail. Being a leader that will effectively change the course in the face of storm require a lot from strategy, understanding of the pattern the wave projects, and being able to garner ideas even from your followers in other to triumph.

I do not want to bore you any much long with my stories, but you are the real gem here, taking your time to read through this book up till this point. But it is important to highlight that my story is a common story and a collation of stories from almost every child living in Africa or better said, living in a sheer difficulty anywhere in the world. It is written to help uplift even if it's one person, to rise up against all odd, in other to make something out of his life. It is a leadership for all and not for fewer.

Every 'Small Me' needs to rise and we will do everything within our reach to make them journey and grow to 'Big Me'.

COACHING POINT:

I want to share this narrative to show you how to leave people to take responsibility in the face of challenges.

I gathered my U16 team together for warm up, and while we were about to start, a player trolled his friend, whom also is playing in the team, and they both started jesting and eventually got me involved. They asked me to have both of them in different teams. Naturally, effective training and practice comes from players most of the times, not only from the coaches. If they are not willing to play, however you motivate them will yield a little. It is like pushing an injured player to play.

So when these friends demanded that they want a challenge against one another, I know it will be one hell of a day in my session. So I obliged.

Firstly, it will make my work easier; I will not need to yell over and over again to get them to do a thing.

Secondly, I do not need to motivate any one of the players as they have come ready.

Thirdly, my support is a vivid approval for them to showcase their inner abilities.

We got on this challengers match, 25 minutes later after warm up and ease drills; I chose the bibs color for red and blue. The red team was for the troller and the blue was for his friends.

I assumed the position of a referee and not necessarily as a coach because at this point, I'm not supposed to interrupt the flow of the game, but I can only take match points and deal with their mistakes later. By the time the game had gotten through half way, the score line was 2 against 1, I yelled out, 2, 1! That was a reminder and a form of motivation.

At the end of a straight 40 minutes intensive match, they were all sweating and breathing profusely and gulping water. It was really high intensity.

The common jesting from two friends change the light of our game from a common dull technique to a tactical high intensity challenge that yield a 3-2 goal line...I will not tell you which team that won...

My match point, the same did not only go to the boys but likewise me, because watching from behind was the director of the academy who enjoyed the whole session with no interfering but then he couldn't hold himself back.

As the boys gathered again, cooling off, awaiting my match-point, a voice came from behind,

"Hello guys!" I turned, it was the club director, "Sorry Edu, I didn't come to take over your beautiful session but I couldn't help it after enjoying the intensity of the game, he smiled, he loves to smile." Who are the captains for the both teams? He asked. The two challenging friends stood up, Bravo! What can you tell us was your formation and tactics while holding to your responsible? gazing at the troller. The troller explained his format, and game pattern with all his tactics, and how he was screaming making sure that every player in his team where holding it together and working harder.

Then his friend before explaining, trolled back at the he troller, "Your team was working harder while we were playing smarter, can you beat that?" We all laughed, and then he explained his own tactics.

Believe me; I was thrown aback at the level of their understanding and knowledge of the game. The energy and the intensity of such evening was a synergy that comes as result individual strengths put together and a challenge of honour as such bring out the leadership in us.

BIBLIOGRAPHY

King James Version Bible.

Brigette hyacinth(2017).The future of leadership; rise of automation, robotic, and artificial intelligence.

Mihaly csikszentmihalyi(1990)   Flow; The psychology of optimal performance

Steven J. Breckler, James M. Olsen, Elizabeth C. Wiggns(2006)Alive; Social Psychology

Ndubisi idejiora kalu (2019)Strategy

HH Shiek Mohammed bin Rashid Al Maktoum(2009)The poems from dessert

Chinedu Darlington (2020).   In the shadow of my mind
Robert T. kiyosaki(2015).   8 lessons in military leadership for entrepreneur.

Robert T. kiyosaki(1997).   Rich Dad, PoorDad(series)

ABOUT THE AUTHOR

Chinedu Darlington, has lived for over a decade in Dubai, United Arab Emirate. He worked as a tech-engineer in a high end luxury multi-sound music system company in his home country. Presently, he is the founder/MD of Darlington Shepherd limited/project; as an entrepreneur, and a proud Asian licensed Football/soccer Coach. He is presently as a youth coach with a private Academy in Dubai. His foundation (Darlington Shepherd project) is inspired to donate school and football materials to children in Africa at the grassroots level in other to support their dreams.

Contact:
c/o Darlington shepherd's project
darlingtonshepherd24@gmail.com

Goodwills to my editors:
Chimkanma Chinazaekepere(Nwachukwu) Chinedu; NIGERIA
Ifechukwu Michaels; AUSTRALIA